SPOTLIGHT ON POETRY

Poems Around the World 1

Contents

Collected by Brian Moses and David Orme

Acknowledgements

Whilst every effort has been made to contact the copyright-holders and to secure the necessary permission to reprint these selections, this has not proved to be possible in every case.

'Water everywhere' by Valerie Bloom, reprinted by permission of the author; 'Sampan' by Tao Lang Pee from Can I Buy a Slice of Sky?: Poems from Black, Asian and American Indian Cultures, edited by Grace Nichols (Blackie, 1991); 'Through the jungle the elephant goes...' from Kiskadee Queen, edited by Faustin Charles (Puffin Books, 1994); 'Everything you do' by Mabel Segun from Under the Mango Tree: Songs and Poems for Primary Schools, edited by Mabel Segun and Neville Grant (Longman, 1980); 'Caribbean Counting Rhyme' by Pamela Mordecai, reprinted by permission of the author; 'Listen' by Telcine Turner from Climbing Clouds: Stories and Poems from the Bahamas, edited by Telcine Turner (Macmillan Caribbean, 1988; 'Goodbye Granny' by Pauline Stewart, reprinted by permission of the author; 'My Sari' by Debjani Chatterjee, reprinted by permission of the author; 'Bed Time' by Accabre Huntley from Easter Monday Blues (Bogle l'Ouverture Press, 1983), reprinted by permission of the publisher; 'The Sea' by Ghadya Parker, reprinted by permission of the author.

The publishers would be pleased to rectify any omissions in the above list brought to their notice at the earliest opportunity.

Published by Collins Educational
An imprint of HarperCollinsPublishers
77-85 Fulham Palace Road
Hammersmith
London W6 8JB

www.**Collins**Education.com
On-line support for schools and colleges

First published 1999

Reprinted 2000

Reprinted 0 9 8 7 6 5 4

ISBN 0 00 310 336 6

Designed by Clare Truscott and Kate Roberts
Cover Design by Clare Truscott and Kate Roberts
Illustrations by Beccy Blake, Basia Bogdanowicz, Bethan Matthews, Jeffrey Reid, Anette Isberg Rosijn, Jan Smith and Lisa Williams

Printed and bound in Great Britain by Scotprint

Collins Educational would like to thank the following teachers and consultants who contributed to the research of this series:

Mrs J. Bibby (St Paul's C of E Primary); Jason Darley, Liz Hooley (Jessop Primary School); Mrs M.G. Farnell (High Meadow First School); Alison Lewis; Chris Lutrario; Lesley Moores (Princess Royal Primary School); Sheila Stamp (Castle Lower School); Sally Prendergrast (Brooke Hill School); Jenny Ransom; Jill Walkinton; Sue Webb; Michael Webster (Castle Lower School); Jill Wells (St Andrews CE Primary School).

Water Everywhere

There's water on the ceiling,
And water on the wall,
There's water in the bedroom,
And water in the hall,
There's water on the landing,
And water on the stair,
Whenever Daddy takes a bath
There's water everywhere.

Valerie Bloom

Sampan

Waves lap lap
Fish fins clap clap
Brown sails flap flap
Chop-sticks tap tap
Up and down the long green river
Ohe Ohe lanterns quiver

Willow branches brush the river
Ohe Ohe lanterns quiver
Waves lap lap
Fish fins clap clap
Brown sails flap flap
Chop-sticks tap tap

Tao Lang Pee

Hey, Elephant

Through the jungle the elephant goes,
Swaying his trunk to and fro,
Munching, crunching, tearing trees,
Stamping seeds, eating leaves.
His eyes are small, his feet are fat,
Hey, elephant, don't behave like that.

Anon.

Listen

Shhhhhhhhhhhhhhhhhhhhhhhhhhhhhhhhhh!
Sit still, very still
And listen.
Listen to wings
Lighter than eyelashes
Stroking the air.
Know what the thin breeze
Whispers on high
To the coconut trees.
Listen and hear.

Telcine Turner

Everything You Do

[first voice]	[second voice]
You shake your head	I shake mine
You wave your hand	I wave mine
You stamp your foot	I stamp mine
You clap your hands	I clap mine
You touch your nose	I touch mine
You pull your ear	I pull mine

You jump in the air
You run on the spot
Everything you do
And wherever you go

I jump too
I run too
I do too
I go too
For I am –
your
shadow!

Mabel Segun

Caribbean Counting Rhyme

One by one
one by one
waves are dancing
in the sun.

Two by two
two by two
seashells pink
and purply-blue.

Three by three
three by three
big boats
putting out to sea.

Four by four
four by four
children fishing
on the shore.

Five by five
five by five
little walking
fish arrive.

Six by six
six by six
pelicans
performing tricks.

Seven by seven
seven by seven
puffy clouds
patrolling heaven.

Eight by eight
eight by eight
fishes nibbling
juicy bait.

Nine by nine
nine by nine
taking home
a catch that's fine.

Ten by ten
ten by ten
tomorrow we
will come again.

Pamela Mordecai

Catch me the Moon, Daddy

Catch me the moon, Daddy,
Let it shine near me awhile.
Catch me the moon, Daddy,
I want to touch its smile.

The moon must shine
From high above;
That's where it needs to stay –
Among the stars,
To guide them home
When they return from play.

And as for you, my child,
With slender silver thread
The moon will weave
Sweet dreams, so you
May slumber in your bed.

Anon.

Goodbye Granny

Goodbye Granny
It's nearly time to fly
goodbye Granny
I am going in the sky.
I have my suitcase
and things.
You have packed
me everything
except the sunshine.

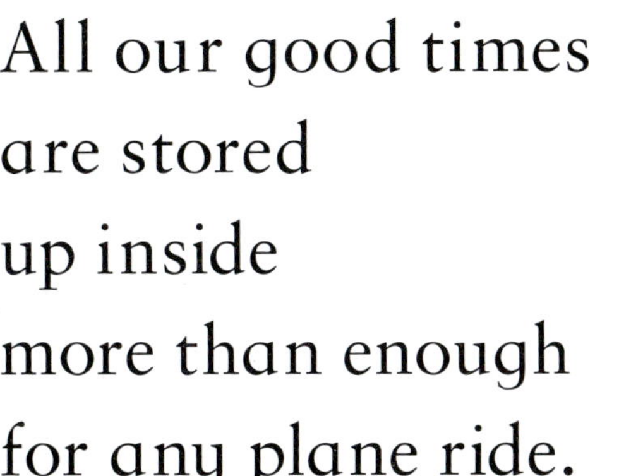

All our good times
are stored
up inside
more than enough
for any plane ride.

Goodbye Granny
things will be all right
goodbye Granny
I won't forget to write.
Goodbye Granny
bye! bye!
bye! bye!

Pauline Stewart

My Sari

Saris hang on the washing line:
a rainbow in our neighbourhood.
This little orange one is mine,
it has a mango leaf design.
I wear it as a Rani would.
It wraps round me like sunshine,
it ripples silky down my spine,
and I stand tall and feel so good.

Debjani Chatterjee

Bed Time

Can I stay up five
minutes more let me
finish this book
Can't I finish this
bead chain
Can't I finish this
castle
        Can't I
        stay up
five minutes or four
three minutes or two
minutes one minute more.

Accabre Huntley

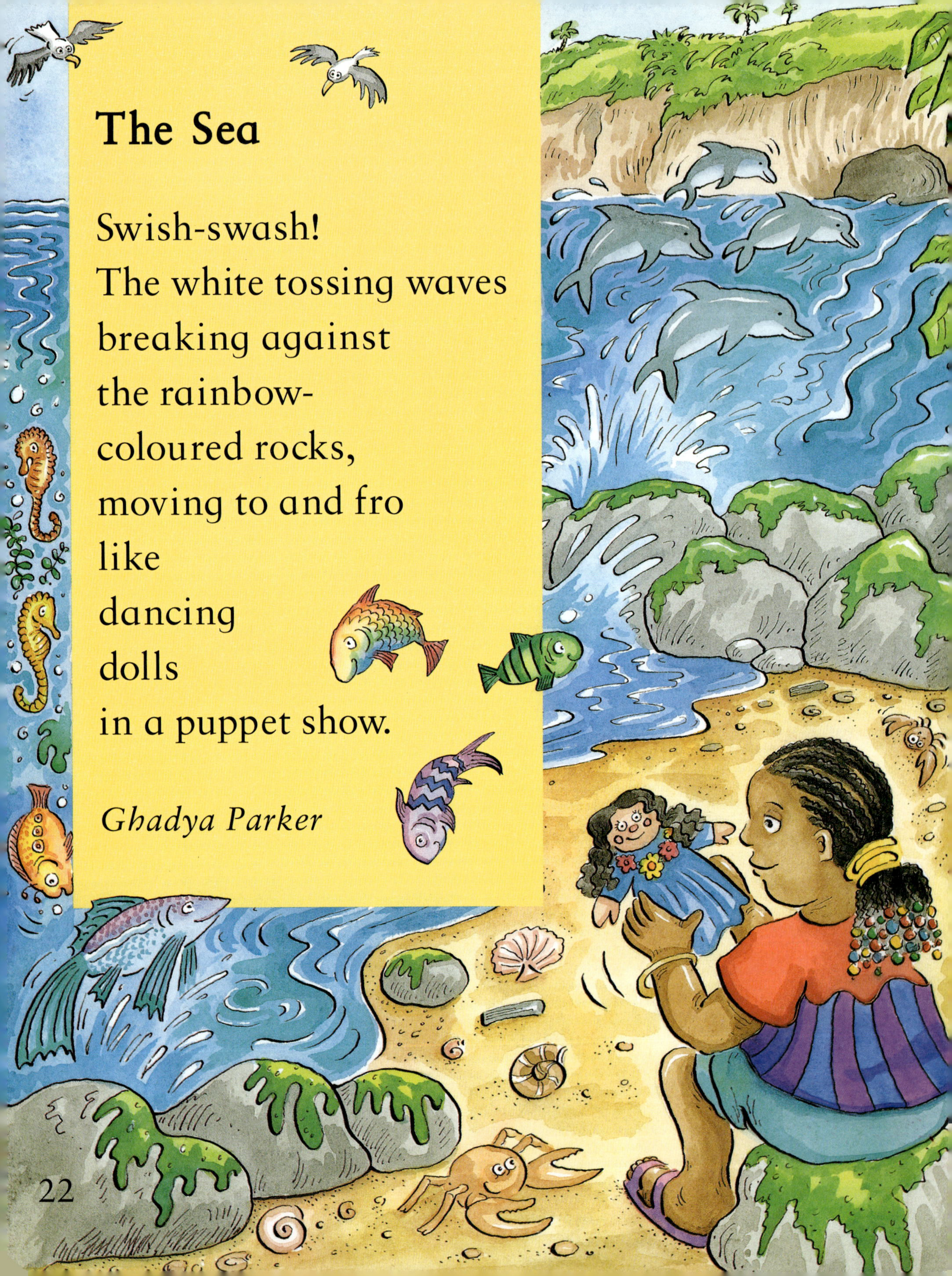

The Sea

Swish-swash!
The white tossing waves
breaking against
the rainbow-
coloured rocks,
moving to and fro
like
dancing
dolls
in a puppet show.

Ghadya Parker

Glossary

Caribbean Counting Rhyme

a catch that's fine big pile of fish caught
juicy bait food to tempt fish
patrolling walking around, looking or guarding
pelicans type of bird

Catch me the Moon, Daddy

awhile for a time
slumber sleep
weave to make cloth

My Sari

Rani an Indian queen or princess, or the wife of a very important person
Sari a long piece of material folded around the body in a special way, can be very decorative

Sampan

chop-sticks a pair of thin sticks used to eat with
lanterns a special light or lamp; it can be made from paper
quiver shake or rustle

Index by title

Index by first line